THE LIFE OF ST. JEROME

Gennadius of Massilia

Translated by: D.P. Curtin

Copyright @ 2022 Dalcassian Publishing Company

All rights reserved. No part of this publication may be reproduced, distributed, or transmitted in any form or by any means, including photocopying, recording, or other electronic or mechanical methods, without the prior written permission of the publisher, except in the case of brief quotations embodied in critical reviews and certain other non-commercial uses permitted by copyright law. For permission request, write to Dalcassian Publishing Company at dalcassianpublishing at gmail.com

ISBN: 978-1-0882-7805-5 (Paperback)

Library of Congress Control Number:
Author: Curtin, D.P. (1985-)

Printed by Ingram Content Group, 1 Ingram Blvd, La Vergne, Tennessee

First printing edition 2022.

THE LIFE OF ST. JEROME

THE LIFE OF ST. JEROME

Our Jerome was born to his father Eusebius in the town of Stridon, which was now overthrown by the Goths, and was once the border of Dalmatia and Pannonia. He took the garment of Christ as a child in Rome, where he was educated in Greek and Latin letters from an early age. Indeed, in the art of Grammar he had Donatus as a teacher, and in Rhetoric Victorinus as an orator. After he had acquired all the literature of worldly studies, he also imitated the behavior and deeds of the most approved monks. Indeed, treading upon the lust of the soul with sincerity, and breaking the pleasure of the body with perpetual fasting, he taught that most of the good and religious men would be better by his institution.

At a certain time, then, while Jerome, as usual, spreads the divine volumes for reading, and remembers Tullius, the mortal author of his library. Soon the celestial, lest he should ever turn over such books, was chastised by a salutary whipping. For thus he himself, writing to the virgin Eustochius, asserts: When many years ago I had cast myself from home, with my parents, my sister, and my relatives, and (which is more difficult for them) by the habit of a more luxurious food, for the sake of the kingdoms of heaven, and I was going to Jerusalem to serve in the army, the library that Rome had with the highest I had done it with study and hard work, and I could not do without it. Thus, wretched I fasted to read Tullius: after the frequent vigils of the night, after the tears, which the remembrance of past sins drew from my bowels (Plautus), Plato was taken in his hands. If I had ever returned to myself, and had begun to read the Prophets, I would have been horrified by the language of the uncultivated; and because I did not see the light with my blind eyes, I thought it was not the fault of the eyes, but of the sun. While the ancient serpent was mocking me, in the middle of Lent, a marrow-infused fever invaded my exhausted body; and without any rest (which is also incredible to say) the unfortunate members were so crushed that they hardly clung to the bones. In the meantime, the funeral was being prepared, and the vital heat of the soul, which was already cold throughout the whole body, was palpitating on the ground, only warming the chest. When I was suddenly carried away in spirit to the judgment-seat, where there was so much light, and so much from the brightness of the surroundings, that I was thrown to the ground, and did not dare to look up. When asked about my condition, I replied that I was a Christian. And he who presided: You lie, said he, you are a Ciceronian, not a

Christian. Where your treasure is, there is your heart. I immediately became speechless, and between the lashes (for he had ordered me to be killed) I was tormented more by the fire of conscience, reciting that verse with myself: But in hell who will confess to you? However, I began to cry, and to say, weeping: Have mercy on me, Lord, have mercy on me. This voice resounded among the whips. At length those who were present fell upon the knees of the president, and prayed that he might grant pardon to youth, and lend a place to repentance for error, and then execute torture, if I had ever read the letters of the Gentiles. , if I ever had secular manuscripts, if I read them, I would deny you. Having dismissed these words of the sacrament, I returned to the superiors; to the astonishment of all, I opened my eyes, drenched in such a shower of tears, that even unbelievers believed out of pain. Nor indeed was that slumber empty, like empty dreams by which we are often deceived. Witness is the tribunal before which I lay, judgment is witness that I feared; so it never happens to me that such a problem occurs. I admit that I had bruised shoulders, and that I felt bruises during the dream; and after that I read with such divine interest that I had not read mortal things before.

In the meantime Jerome, the priest of the Roman Church, the mouth of the priest of Damasus, the searcher of the sacred library, the interpreter of the divine volumes, while for three continuous years he was dear and accepted by the popular people, and in the judgment of all was judged to be worthy of the high priesthood, some of the orders of the clerics and monks, arguing for petulance and indecency, to flee the city of Jerome , who had discovered the faults of both of them by writing, prepared a plot. For indeed I would call this one happy, correcting the event of this flight, dispensed by the judgment of Christ, whom I think would be prepared for the persecutions of wicked men: namely, as the Roman Church, under the rule established by Peter, and taught the truth of all the books of the Old Testament, willing to Christ God, and betraying Jerome with a special zeal , may also have a Hebrew truth; and the levity of some of the Greeks, who flattered themselves that the Romans had received from them all the Scriptures divinely inspired, acknowledges that they have what they do not have. Therefore, Jerome leaving Rome, heading eastward, went to Gregory Nazianzen, bishop of the city of Constantinople; where he strove to make such progress that he was gifted with wonderful knowledge. He, that he might be thoroughly educated in the study of the holy Scriptures, a supple and docile pupil, went to this teacher, and observed him in the city of Constantinople. When Jerome had completed this discipleship, he went into Syria: and while he was staying in the possession of the priest Evagrius, he found Malchus the Monk, sometimes a prisoner, and having questioned him, he received the whole history of his captivity, which he afterwards published and wrote and sent to the Roman faithful, interspersing these in the prologue of his history. I have resolved to write, says he, if God will give me life, and if my accusers will at least cease to persecute me as I fled and was shut up. Then he came to the deserted places, to which he had longed to hasten to do penance there, so joyfully and girded himself that you would have thought he had flown rather than returned. But how for four continuous years he had rather repented with the help of Christ, the same Jerome who had suffered voluntarily (al. suffered), he indicated that the grace of God himself was present with words of this kind. Whenever I was stationed in the desert, and that vast wilderness, which, scorched by the heat of the sun, affords monastics a hideous habitation, I thought to myself, says he, participating in the pleasures of the Romans. I sat alone because I was filled with bitterness. The disfigured limbs of the sack shuddered; the squalid skin had brought the place of the Ethiopian flesh. Daily tears, daily groans; and if at any time the threatening sleep had oppressed me, I would have struck the naked ground with scarcely adhering bones. But I am silent about food and drink, since even those who are sick there use cold water, and to have received something cooked is a luxury. I, then, who for fear of hell had condemned myself to such a prison, was only a companion of scorpions and beasts, often joined the choirs of girls. Their mouths were pale with fasting, and their minds were heated with desires: in their cold body, and before their man the flesh was already dead, only the fires of lust were sprouting. And so, despondent of all help, I lay at Jesus' feet, watered myself with tears, wiped my hair, and subjected my resistant flesh to weeks of hunger. I am not ashamed of my unhappiness, but rather lament that I am not what I was. I remember that I often joined the day and the night crying and did not cease from the beatings of my chest before the Lord's commanding calmness returned. I was also afraid of my own cell, as if I were conscious of my thoughts: and angry and rigid with myself I entered the desert alone. Wherever I saw hollow valleys, rugged mountains, precipitous cliffs, there I placed myself in prayer as a prisoner of the most miserable flesh; and (as the Lord is my witness) after many tears, with eyes fixed behind heaven, I sometimes saw myself participating in the processions of angels; and I sang joyfully and joyfully: We run after you in the scent of your perfumes.

Accordingly, after four years of dedicated penance, Jerome returned to the town of Bethlehem, where the wise animal offered himself to remain at the manger of the Lord. Having closed his library, which he himself had prepared for himself with the greatest zeal, and the prayers of all the books, which he kept almost by heart, he re-read them again, and led the day fasting until the evening. Many of the Religious, who had heard the fame of his life, immediately flocked to him; And not much after the cell, because of the number of disciples, and because of the frequency of those who came to the gate of Bethlehem, which looks to the West, and to those who go out it is seen to the North, he built a small dwelling-room.

In the meantime, while Jerome was surveying the humble and subterranean dwellings of the excellent Hermits and Monks, he was divulging their lives with the voice of the executed, and in writing he expounded the truth; blessed Damasus, the most eloquent Pontiff of the Church of the Roman city, was exhorted in such words as to not cease from constant work in writing and sending volumes to his own Church of the Roman city. To his beloved son Hieronymus Damasus. I have arranged to awaken you, who were sleeping, and who for a long time had been reading rather than writing, by sending you questions; but that this is the fruit of reading, if you write. And since, when I sent the courier to you, you said that you no longer had any letters, except those which you had once dictated in the desert, and which I read and wrote with all avidity, and you further promised that I could dictate some of them by the stealthy works of the night if I wished: I gladly accept from the offerer, that I wanted to ask, even if you refused. For I do not think that there would be any kind of conversation more worthy of our discussion, than that we should talk about the Scriptures among ourselves, that is, that I should ask, and you should answer, in which life I think there is nothing more delightful in this light, in which the soul's fodder surpasses all honey. How sweet, says the Prophet, are your words in my throat! upon the honey of my mouth. For since, as the chief speaker says, let us distinguish men from the beasts, we can speak: what praise is he who excels the rest in that matter, in which men excel the beasts? So that I should also circumscribe those things which are subject to me, keeping control on both sides, so that neither the proposals should be wanting in solution, nor the Epistle brevity. Indeed, I confess to you that the books which you gave me on the subject of Lactantius, I therefore do not gladly read, because most of his Epistles extend to the space of a thousand lines, and he rarely discusses our dogma; and if they are short, they are more suitable for scholars than for us, discussing meters, and the situation of regions and philosophers.

What does it mean that it is written in Genesis: Whoever kills Cain will pay seven vengeances. But even if God made all things very good, why does he command Noah about clean and unclean animals, since nothing unclean can be good? And in the New Testament, after the vision which had been shown to Peter, saying: Abstain, Lord, for the common and unclean has never entered my mouth, a voice from heaven answered: What the Lord God has cleansed, then do not say common.

Why does God speak to Abraham, saying that the fourth generation of the children of Israel were to return from Egypt; and afterwards Moses wrote: Now in the fifth generation or seed the children of Israel came out of the land of Egypt. Which of course, unless explained, seems to be the opposite. Why did Abraham accept the sign of Circumcision? Why did Isaac, just and dear to God, bless not whom he willed, but whom he did not want, deceived by error?

Now by what ventures and how many labors Jerome, alone of all the Romans, learned the Hebrew language and letters, nay, the Chaldaic language, as he himself went through, it must be connected: While I was young, he says, and I was surrounded by deserts, encouraged by vices, and I could not bear the ardor of nature (al. what); which, when I had broken frequent fasts, my mind was nevertheless heated with thoughts. To whom, to tame, a certain brother who had believed from the Hebrews, I gave myself as a pupil: that after the acumen of Quintilian, the river of Cicero, the gravity of Fronton, and the gentleness of Pliny, I might learn the alphabet, and meditate on the shrill and panting words. What labors I undertook there, what hardships I endured, how often I despaired, and how often I ceased, my conscience is witness, who suffered, and those who led their lives with me. And thanks be to God, that from the bitter seed of literature I get sweet fruits. Moreover, the book of Job, written indeed in Hebrew letters, but indeed in the Chaldean language, when Jerome translated it into Latin, he who is attached below, had as his teacher: Remember me, he says, for the intelligence of this volume, a certain teacher

Lyddaeus, who was considered the first among the Hebrews, not small having paid back the money I do not know if I have learned anything from his teaching: this one thing I know, that I could not have been interpreted except by what I had previously understood. By what labor and sweat he learned the Chaldean language, says Jerome, writing and affirming the same. I, a young man, after the reading of Quintilian and Tullius, and the flowers of Rhetoric, when I had shut myself up in the tongues of this bakery, and, with much sweat and for a long time, had begun to echo panting and shrill words, and as if walking through a crypt, looking at a rare light from above, I at last turned upon Daniel, and with so much weariness I am, so that in a sudden despair I would wish to despise all my old labors. But the Hebrew man exhorting me and instilling in me more often with his own tongue, that toil conquers all, the wicked one, who seemed to me to be the wisest among them, I began again to be a Chaldean disciple. And to be more truthful, to this day I can read and understand the Chaldean language more than I can sound it. Therefore, by the grace of Christ, Jerome, having obtained faith, and having learned Greek, Latin, and Hebrew letters, translated all the volumes of the Hebrews contained in the Canon, from the Old Testament, the true Edition, into the Latin language, and commented on them all. He also described Daniel as speaking the Chaldean language in Roman style. To wit, the psalter which Jerome had requested from Sophronius to be sung from the Hebrew Canon in Latin tuning, he expounded word for word, and briefly discussed it and called it an enchiridion. He expounded the two books of Solomon: the Song of Songs, with Origen's interpretation: just as he translated the book of the seer of the Holy Spirit of Didymus into the Latin language. Matthew nevertheless made the Gospel from the Hebrew to be Roman; and this was interpreted by a concise rather than a fastidious explanation to the studious readers. Also, sixteen volumes or prophecies of the Prophets were found to have been remembered or begun to be written by none of the Romans; he argued that they were published in seventy-four books. Moreover, he discussed most of the Epistles of Paul and the revelation of John. And so among these numerous pages of his work, prefaced by his entire prefaces, he arranged in order five hundred and thirty illustrious men ecclesiastical writers from the passion of Christ to the fourteenth year of the Emperor Theodosius, and all who have handed down something of the sacred Scriptures to memory. he explained briefly. True, and against Celsus, Porphyry, and Julian Augustus, rabid dogs against Christ, and against the insectists of the Church, or those who think that the Church has had no philosophers and eloquent teachers, he perspired with great ingenuity: that they may know how many and what kind of men founded it, built it, and adorned it: and let them cease to accuse our faith of rustic simplicity, and rather recognize their own inexperience.

In addition to the innumerable constructions of the books of the Apostles and Prophets: and after a little, now also the mystery of iniquity works. And each one murmurs what he feels: I am the only one who is bitten by the glory of others. Finally, he was so exhausted by fatigue that even lying on his bed, he was raised by a rope hanging from a beam and holding his back by his hands; that is to say, to present the duty of the Monastery as best he could, passing most of the days in squalor of body and feebleness of voice. Henceforth Jerome, supported by an abundance of books, and dedicated to his words to the Holy Spirit, loosened the immovable tower of the Catholic Church against the arrows of the perfidious, against the Helvidius, against the Pelagius, and against the Jovinians, with the most evident volumes, fortified with Catholic rebuke, and written with great acuity; and published a thundering book. He weaves the lives of most of the Hermit Fathers with the most truthful expression of history. He also wrote one book about the mansions of the Israelite people; For he explained the story of the Gospel about the rich and luxurious son in an elegant way, and explained it with such comforting discourses that it is thought to be unique. For to many, says he, who say that I write this work inflamed with the flames of envy, I answer briefly, that I have never spared heretics; but that he acted with all diligence, that the enemies of the Church should become my enemies also.

The older Catholics therefore continued to visit and comfort Jerome while he was in labor. To the blessed Bishop Augustine, who was indeed cooperating with his mind in the Catholic Church, but writing with his body in Africa, he wrote in this way among others: We have had our times, we have run as far as we could; Therefore Jerome, who as a young man had vowed to Christ God, offered this perfect life to him now in his old body, chaste, agreeable, unique in the Bethlehemite penitence in the wilderness. Moreover, he filled the whole world with his books for six and fifty years without any rest among the people of Bethlehem. Bethlehem holds him dear, to be offered to the Lord again when he comes. Blessed Jerome fell asleep in the 12th year of the reign of Theodosius the Younger. All the years of his life are thus collected. He was ordained priest of Rome at the age of twenty-nine, lived three years at Bethlehem, and in his purpose fifty years and six months. He filled all the time of his life with 88 years and six months. He fell asleep in the Lord on the first day of October.

LATIN TEXT

Hieronymus noster in oppido Stridonis, quod a Gothis nunc eversum, Dalmatiae quondam Pannoniaeque confinium fuit, patre Eusebio natus est. Vestem Christi puer Romae suscepit, ibique litteris Graecis ac Latinis a primaevo eruditus est. In arte quidem Grammatica Donatum habuit praeceptorem, in Rhetorica autem Victorinum oratorem. Postquam vero omnem mundanorum studiorum litteraturam adeptus est, probatissimorum quoque Monachorum habitum factumque imitatus est. Cupiditatem siquidem animae jugi sinceritate calcans voluptatemque corporis perenni frangens jejunio, plerosque virorum bonorum et religiosorum meliores fore suo docuit instituto.

Quodam igitur tempore, dum ex more idem Hieronymus, divina ad legendum pandit volumina, et mortalem bibliothecae suae auctorem Tullium recordatur. Mox coelitus, ne tales quandoque revolveret libros, salutifero castigatus est verbere. Ita enim ipse de se ad Eustochium virginem scribens asserit: Cum ante annos plurimos domo, parentibus, sorore, cognatis, et (quod his difficilius est) consuetudine lautioris cibi propter coelorum me regna castrassem, et Jerosolymam militaturus pergerem, bibliotheca, quam Romae cum summo studio ac labore confeceram, carere non poteram. Ita miser ego lecturus Tullium jejunabam: post noctium crebras vigilias, post lacrymas, quas mihi praeteritorum recordatio peccatorum ex imis visceribus eruebat (Plautus), Plato sumebatur in manibus. Si quando in memetipsum reversus, Prophetas legere coepissem, sermo horrebat incultus; et quia lumen caecis oculis non videbam, non oculorum culpam putabam, sed solis. Dum me (al. ita) itaque antiquus serpens illuderet, in media ferme Quadragesima medullis infusa febris corpus meum invasit exhaustum; et sine ulla requie (quod dictu quoque incredibile sit) sic infelicia membra depasta sunt, ut ossibus vix haererent. Interim parabantur exequiae, et vitalis animi calor, toto frigescente jam corpore, in solo tantum tepente pectusculo palpitabat. Cum subito raptus in spiritu ad tribunal judicis pertrahor, ubi tantum luminis, et tantum erat ex circumstantium claritate fulgoris, ut projectus in terram, sursum aspicere non auderem. Interrogatus conditionem, Christianum me esse respondi. Et ille qui praesidebat: Mentiris, ait, Ciceronianus es, non Christianus. Ubi thesaurus tuus, ibi et cor tuum est. Illico obmutui, et inter verbera (nam caedi me jusserat) conscientiae igne magis torquebar, illum mecum versiculum reputans: In inferno autem quis confitebitur tibi? Clamare tamen coepi, et ejulans dicere: Miserere mei, Domine, miserere mei. Haec vox inter flagella resonabat. Tandem ad praesidentis genua provoluti qui assistebant precabantur, ut veniam tribueret adolescentiae, et errori locum poenitentiae commodaret, exacturus deinde cruciatum, si gentilium litterarum aliquando legissem: Ego qui tanto constrictus articulo vellem etiam majora promittere, dejerare coepi, et nomen ejus obtestans dicere: Domine, si unquam habuero codices saeculares, si legero, te negavi. In haec sacramenti verba dimissus revertor ad superos; mirantibus cunctis, oculos aperio tanto lacrymarum imbre perfusos, ut etiam incredulis fidem facerem ex dolore. Nec vero sopor ille inanis fuit, ut vana somnia, quibus saepe deludimur. Teste est tribunal ante quod jacui, judicium teste quod timui; ita mihi nunquam contingat talem incidere quaestionem. Livientes (sup. fateor) me habuisse scapulas, plagas sensisse per somnium; et tanto dehinc studio divina legisse, quanto mortalia antea non legeram.

Interea Hieronymus Romanae Ecclesiae Presbyter, os Damasi Sacerdotis, sacrae Bibliothecae scrutator, divinorum dissertor voluminum, dum per triennium continuum carus acceptusque popularibus veneratur, omniumque judicio dignus esse summo sacerdotio decernitur, quidam ex Clericorum Monachorum ordinibus pro petulantia proque ingluvie discursantes, ad effugandum Urbe Hieronymum, qui utrorumque eorum vitia scribens deprehenderat, insidias paraverunt. Verum enim vero hunc ego felicem dixerim, hujus fugae eventum corrigentis, Christi judicio dispensatum, quem pravorum hominum persecutionibus paratum fore existimo: scilicet ut Romana Ecclesia, Petri instituta regimine, omniumque veteris Testamenti librorum edocta veritate, Christo Deo volente, et Hieronymi speciali studio desudante, Hebraicam quoque habeat veritatem; et Graecorum quorumdam levitas, quae sibi Romanos a se omnes Scripturas divinitus inspiratas accepisse plaudebat, eos habere quod non habet, recognoscat. Igitur Hieronymus Roma egressus, ad orientem tendens, profectus est ad Gregorium Nazianzenum Constantinopolitanae urbis Episcopum; ubi ita proficere studuit, ut mira scientia donaretur. Qui ut sanctarum Scripturarum studiis plene erudiretur,

supplex docilisque discipulus hunc adiit praeceptorem, eumque
Constantinopolitana urbe observabat. Hoc discipulatu Hieronymus peracto,
in Syriam perrexit: et dum in possessione Evagrii presbyteri moraretur,
Malchum Monachum et aliquando captivum reperit, percunctatusque eum,
omnem ejus captivitatis accepit historiam, quam postea edidit scriptam et
Romanis fidelibus misit, haec in ejus historiae prologo interserens. Scribere,
inquit, disposui, si tamen Deus vitam dederit, et si vituperatores mei saltem
fugientem me et clausum persequi desierint. Ad deserta deinde loca, ad quae
olim ad agendam inibi poenitentiam properare cupierat, ita laetus
accinctusque accessit, ut volasse eum magis quam remeasse crederes.
Quomodo vero per quadriennium continuum Christi potius auxilio
poenituerit, idem Hieronymus quae sponte (al. pertulit) pertulerit, ipsius Dei
adfuisse gratiam verbis hujusmodi indicavit. Quoties in eremo constitutus, et
illa vasta solitudine, quae exusta solis ardoribus horridum Monachis praestat
habitaculum, putavi me, inquit, Romanis interesse deliciis. Sedebam solus quia
amaritudine repletus eram. Horrebant sacco membra deformia; squalida cutis
situm Aethiopicae carnis adduxerat. Quotidie lacrymae, quotidie gemitus; et si
aliquando repugnantem somnus imminens oppressisset, nuda humo vix ossa
haerentia collidebam. De cibis vero et potu taceo, cum etiam languentes ibi
aqua frigida utantur, et coctum aliquid accepisse, luxuriae sit. Ille igitur ego,
qui ob metum gehennae tali me carcere ipse damnaveram, scorpionum
tantum socius et ferarum, saepe choris intereram puellarum. Pallebant ora
jejuniis, et mens desideriis aestuabat. In frigido corpore, et ante hominem
suum jam carne praemortua, sola libidinum incendia pullulabant. Itaque omni
auxilio destitutus, ad Jesu jacebam pedes, rigabam lacrymis, crine tergebam, et
repugnantem carnem hebdomadarum inedia subigebam. Non erubesco
infelicitatis meae, quin potius plango non esse quod fuerim. Memini me
clamantem diem crebro junxisse cum nocte, nec prius a pectoris cessasse
verberibus, quam a Domino rediret imperante tranquillitas. Ipsam quoque
cellulam meam quasi cogitationum consciam pertimescebam: et mihi iratus et
rigidus solus deserta penetrabam. Sicubi concava vallium, aspera montium,
rupium praerupta cernebam, ibi me in oratione miserrimae carnis ergastulo
locabam; et (ut mihi testis est Dominus) post multas lacrymas, post coelo
oculos inhaerentes, nonnunquam videbar mihi interesse agminibus

Angelorum; et laetus gaudensque cantabam: Post te in odorem unguentorum tuorum currimus.

Quadriennio itaque dedicatae poenitentiae (al. exactae) exacto, ad Bethleem oppidum Hieronymus remeavit, ubi prudens animal ad praesepe Domini sese obtulit permansurum. Bibliothecam suam quam sibi summo studio ipse condiderat, clausam, omniumque librorum orationes, quas pene memoriter retinebat, iterum relegens, diem jejunans ducebat ad vesperam. Plures ad eum Religiosorum, quibus vitae ejus fama comperta erat, protinus confluxerunt: bonumque Doctorem parvo adhuc sub tugurio boni observavere discipuli. Nec multum post cellulam sibi ob discipulorum copiam, et propter frequentiam adventantium ad Bethleemiticam portam, quae ad Occidentem conspicit, et egredientibus ad Septentrionem videtur, parvulum habitationis locellum construxit.

Interim Hieronymus dum eximiorum Eremitarum, Monachorumque humilia subterraneaque peragrans habitacula contemplatur, vitasque eorum supplici voce sciscitans, scribensque veritatem exponit, multaque alia libellis suis, epistolisque suo in Monasterio conficiens edisserit; beatus Damasus Romanae urbis Ecclesiae eloquentissimus Pontifex, ut ad suam idem Romanae urbis Ecclesiam, ad scribenda mittendaque volumina assiduo opere non desisteret, hujusmodi verbis exhortatus est. Dilectissimo filio Hieronymo Damasus. Dormitantem te, et longo jam tempore legentem potius quam scribentem, quaestiunculis ad te missis excitare disposui: non quo legere non debeas, hoc enim veluti quotidiano cibo alitur et pinguescit oratio; sed quod lectionis fructus sit iste, si scribas. Itaque quoniam et tabellario ad te remisso, nullas te jam habere Epistolas dixisti, exceptis his quas in eremo aliquando dictaveras, quasque tota aviditate legi atque scripsi, et ultro pollicitus es, furtivis noctium operibus aliquas si velim posse dictare: libenter accipio ab offerente, quod rogare volueram, etiam si negasses. Neque enim ullam puto digniorem disputationis nostrae confabulationem fore, quam ut de Scripturis inter nos sermocinemur, id est, ut ego interrogem, tu respondeas, qua vita nihil in hac luce puto jucundius, quo animae pabulo omnia mella superantur. Quam dulcia, inquit Propheta, gutturi meo eloquia tua! super mel ori meo. Nam cum idcirco, ut ait praecipuus Orator, homines a bestiis differamus, quod loqui possumus: qua laude dignus est, qui in ea re caeteros superat, in qua homines bestiis antecellunt? Accingere igitur et mihi quae subjecta sunt edissere, servans utrobique moderamen, ut nec proposita solutionem desiderent, nec Epistola brevitatem. Fateor quippe tibi, quia libros quos mihi de fiae Lactantii dederas, ideo non libenter lego, quia plurimae Epistolae ejus usque ad mille versuum spatia tenduntur, et raro de nostro dogmate disputat: quo fit, ut et legenti fastidium generet longitudo; et si qua brevia sunt, scholasticis magis sunt apta quam nobis. De metris, et regionum situ et Philosophis disputans.

Quid sibi vult quod in Genesi scriptum est: Omnis qui occiderit Cain, septem vindictas solvet. Sed et si onmia fecit Deus bona valde, quare ad Noe de mundis et immundis animalibus mandat, cum immundum nihil bonum esse possit? Et in novo Testamento post visionem quae Petro fuerat ostensa dicenti: Absit, Domine, quia commune et immundum nunquam introivit in os meum, vox de coelo respondit: Quod Dominus Deus mundavit, tunc commune ne dixeris.

Cur Deus ad Abraham loquitur dicens, quod quarta progenie filii Israel de Aegypto essent reversuri; et postea Moyses scripsit: Quinta autem generatione vel progenie exierunt filii Israel de terra Aegypti. Quod utique nisi exponatur, videtur esse contrarium. Cur Abraham signum Circumcisionis suscepit? Cur Isaac justus et Deo carus, non illi cui voluit, sed cui noluit deceptus errore benedixit?

Nunc quibus ausibus quantisque laboribus solus omnium Romanorum Hieronymus, Hebraicam linguam litterasque, imo Chaldaicam linguam didicerit, sicut ipse perhibuit, subnectendum est: Dum essem, inquit, juvenis, et solitudinis me deserta vallarent, incentiva vitiorum, ardoremque naturae ferre non poteram (al. quae); quem quum crebris jejuniis trangerem, mens tamen cogitationibus aestuabat. Ad quem edomandum, cuidam fratri, qui ex Hebraeis crediderat, me in discipulum dedi: ut post Quintiliani acumina, Ciceronis fluvium, gravitatemque Frontonis, et lenitatem Plinii, alphabetum discerem, stridentia anhelantiaque verba meditarer. Quid ibi laboris insumpserim, quid sustinuerim difficultatis, quoties desperaverim, quotiesque cessaverim, testis est conscientia mea, qui passus sum, quam eorum qui mecum duxerunt vitam. Et gratias Deo, quod de amaro semine litterarum, dulces fructus capio. Porro librum Job Hebraicis quidem litteris, sed Chaldaico quidem sermone conscriptum, cum Hieronymus verteret in Latinum, hunc qui subter adnexus est, habuit praeceptorem: Memini me, inquit, ob intelligentiam hujus voluminis, Liddeum quemdam praeceptorem, qui apud Hebraeos primus habebatur, non parvis redemisse nummis. Si ejus doctrina aliquid profecerim, nescio: hoc unum scio, non potuisse me nisi quod antea intellexeram, interpretari. Quo vero labore sudoreque Chaldaeam linguam didicerit, idem Hieronymus ita scribens, atque adfirmans dicit. Ego adolescentulus post Quintiliani et Tullii lectionem ac flores Rhetoricos, cum me in linguae hujus pistrinum reclusissem, et multo sudore multoque tempore coepissem anhelantia stridentiaque verba resonare, et quasi per cryptam ambulans, rarum desuper lumen aspicere, impegi novissime in Danielem, et tanto taedio affectus sum, ut desperatione subita omnem veterem laborem voluerim contemnere. Verum adhortante me viro Hebraeo, et illud mihi sua lingua crebrius ingerente, labor omnia vincit improbus, qui mihi videbar sciolus inter eos, coepi rursus discipulus esse Chaldaicus. Et ut verius fatear, usque in praesentem diem magis possum sermonem Chaldaicum legere et intelligere, quam sonare. Christi itaque gratia Hieronymus fidem adeptus, litterisque Graecis ac Latinis atque Hebraicis doctus, cuncta Hebraeorum volumina, quae in Canone continentur, ex veteri Testamento, vera Editione in linguam Latinam vertit, eaque omnia commentatus est. Danielem quoque Chaldaico sermone locutum Romano stylo descripsit. Psalterium videlicet quod a Soffronio postulatus Hieronymus ex Hebraeo Canone Latina modulatione canendum, verbum ad verbum exposuit, eumque breviter disseruit et enchiridionem appellavit. Duos libros Salomonis explanavit: Cantica vero Canticorum ex Origenis interpretatione: sicut et de Spiritu Sancto Didymi videntis librum in Latinam transtulit linguam. Matthaei nihilominus Evangelium ex Hebraeo fecit esse Romanum; quodque compendiosa potius quam fastidiosa explanatione studiosis lectoribus interpretatus est. Sexdecim quoque Prophetarum volumina seu vaticinia a nullo quandoque Romanorum vel meminisse vel scribere inchoasse reperta, disseruit quatuor et septuaginta libris editos Commentatus est. Plerasque praeterea Pauli Epistolas, et Joannis revelationem disseruit. Inter has itaque numerosas operis sui paginas, suis (al. universis) universas praefationibus praenotatas, quinque et centum triginta Virorum Illustrium Ecclesiasticos scriptores a passione Christi usque ad quartum decimum Theodosii Imperatoris annum, in ordinem digessit, omnesque qui de Scripturis sanctis memoriae aliquid tradiderunt, breviter exposuit. Verum et contra Celsum, Porphyrium, et Julianum Augustum, rabidos adversus Christum canes, et contra insectatores Ecclesiae, vel eos qui putant Ecclesiam nullos Philosophos et eloquentes habuisse doctores, magno suda vit ingenio: ut sciant quanti et quales viri eam fundaverint, exstruxerint, adornaverint: et desinant fidem nostram rusticae simplicitatis arguere, suamque potius imperitiam recognoscere.

Innumeris praeterea libris Apostolorum Prophetarum constructionibus: et post pauca, nunc quoque mysterium iniquitatis operatur. Et garrit unusquisque quod sentit: ego solus sum qui cunctorum gloria mordear. Tanta denique lassitudine fatigatus est, ut etiam in stratu suo jacens, funiculo trabe suspenso, supinisque manibus apprehenso erigeretur; ut scilicet officium Monasterii prout poterat exhiberet, transeuntes in squalore corporis, vocisque tenuitate dies plurimi. Dehinc Hieronymus librorum abundantia fultus, dictis suis Sancto (Al. Spiritu) Spiritui dedicatis, immobilem Catholicae Ecclesiae turrem contra perfidorum jacula, contra Helvidium, contraque Pelagium, et adversus Jovinianum evidentissima volumina, Catholicaque correptione roborata, magnoque scripta acumine laxavit: juris quoque consultus singularem tonantemque edidit librum. Plerasque Eremitarum Patrum vitas insignium veracissimo eloquio texuit historiae. De Mansionibus quoque Israelitici populi scripsit librum unum; Namque de frugi et luxurioso filio eleganter exposuit Evangelii historiam, ita consolatoriis dissertionibus declaravit, ut unicam fore arbitretur. Plurimis quippe, ait, qui me dicunt hoc opus inflammatum invidiae facibus scribere, breviter respondeo, nunquam me haereticis pepercisse; sed omni egisse studio, ut hostes Ecclesiae, mei quoque hostes fierent.

Pergunt itaque ad visitandum, consolandumque Hieronymum, dum in labore esset (Al. idem) identidem Catholici seniores. Ad Beatum quoque Augustinum Episcopum secum quidem animo in Ecclesia Catholica cooperantem, corpore autem in Africa scribentem, sic in caetera scripsit: Nostra habuimus tempora, cucurrimus quantum potuimus: nunc te currente et longo spatia transmittente, nobis debetur otium. Igitur Hieronymus, quam Christo Deo adolescens voverat, hanc perfectam eidem jam corpore senex obtulit vitam suam, castam, placibilem, unicam in eremo poenitentiam Bethleemiticam. Libris praeterea suis per sex et quinquaginta annos sine ullo otio apud Bethleemiticos, totum implevit orbem, spiritali opere irreprehensibiliter consummatis, octavo et octogesimo aetatis suae anno in Domino requievit. Bethleem eum alma tenet, iterum venturo Domino offerendum. Dormivit autem Beatus Hieronymus anno imperii Theodosii junioris 12. Omnes autem anni vitae ejus sic colliguntur. Ordinatus est Romae Presbyter annorum viginti novem, annis tribus vixit apud Bethleem, in proposito suo annis quinquaginta et mensibus sex. Omne vitae suae tempus implevit 88 annis et mensibus sex. Dormivit in Domino pridie kalendas Octobris.

The Scriptorium Project is the work of a small group of lay people of various apostolic churches who are interested in the preservation, transmission, and translation of the works of the early and medieval church. Our efforts are to make the works of the church fathers accessible to anyone who might have an interest in Christian antiquities and the theological, philosophical, and moral writings that have become the bedrock of Western Civilization.

To-date, our releases have pulled from the Greek, Syriac, Georgian, Latin, Celtic, Ethiopian, and Coptic traditions of Christianity, and have been pulled from sundry local traditions and languages.

Other Titles and Translations by D.P. Curtin:

Lebor Gabala Erenn by Nennius the Monk (2017)
The Eight Vices by Eutropis of Valencia (2017)
Three Letters from the Companion of the Bulgars by St. Rupert of Juvavum (2017)
Privileges of the Abbot of Canterbury by St. Augustine of Canterbury (2017)
Chapters on Church Law by Pope Adrian I (2017)
A Song of Aethelwolf by Aethelwolf of Lindisfarne (2017)
Humility & Obedience by Novatus the Catholic (2017)
Nicene Canons in the Old Nubian Language (2018)
Apology to Gunthamund, King of Vandals by Aemeilius Dracontius (2018)
Fragments by St. Ephraim of Antioch (2018)
An Account of the Gallican Liturgy by St. Germain of Paris (2018)
Visigothic Chronicle by John of Biclaro (2018)
Preludes by Photius of Paris (2018)
First Book of Ethiopian Maccabees (2018)
Chronicon: a short chronicle of Visigothic Spain by Eutrandus of Ticino (2019)
Decrees of Aethelbert by St. Aethelbert, King of Kent (2019)
The Measure to be taxed for Penance by St. Columba of Iona (2019)
The Privileges of Rome by Louis I the Pious (2019)
Protoevangelium of James: Greek and English Texts (2019)
Edicts of the Synod of Paris by Chlothar II, King of Franks (2019)
The Synod of Rome by St. Boniface IV of Rome (2019)
Letter to Pope Theodore by Victor of Carthage (2020)
The Decree of 610 by Gundemar, King of Visigoths (2020)
Laws of the Church by Chlothar III, King of Franks (2020)
Donations by St. Aethelbert, King of Kent (2020)
The Mystical Interpretation by St. Aileran the Wise (2020)
Laws of the Church by St. Dagobert II, King of Franks (2020)
The Old Nubian Miracle of St. Mena (2021)
Council of Seleucia-Ctesiphon by Mar Isaac of Seleucia (2021)
A Book of Placesnames from 'Acts' by St. Jerome (2021)
About Fifteen Problems by St. Albertus Magnus (2022)
Testament of Some Former Things by John Scotus Eriugena (2022)
The Georgian Synaxarium (2022)
Instructions: Counsel for Novices by St. Ammonas the Hermit (2022)
The Syriac Menologium and Martyrology (2022)
Book on Religious Exercise and Quiet by St. Isaiah the Solitary (2022)
Vision of Theophilus by St. Cyril of Alexandria (2022)
On Fate (De Fato) by St. Albertus Magnus (2023)
Fragments of 'Chronicle' by Hippolytus of Thebes (2023)
Life of the Blessed Theotokos by Epiphanius Monachus (2023)
Syriac Life of John the Baptist by Serapion the Presbyter (2023)